SING,
WRESTLE,
SPIN

SING, WRESTLE, SPIN

Prayers for Active Kids

JENNIFER GRANT

Morehouse Publishing
NEW YORK

Morehouse Publishing, 19 East 34th Street, New York, NY 10016

Morehouse Publishing is an imprint of Church Publishing Incorporated.

Cover design by Jennifer Kopec, 2Pug Design
Interior illustrations by Gillian Whiting
Interior design/typesetting by Beth Oberholtzer

Library of Congress Cataloging-in-Publication Data

Names: Grant, Jennifer, author.
Title: Sing, wrestle, spin : prayers for active kids / Jennifer Grant.
Description: New York, NY : Morehouse Publishing, [2022] | Audience: Ages 7-11 | Audience: Grades 4-6
Identifiers: LCCN 2021048218 (print) | LCCN 2021048219 (ebook) | ISBN 9781640655164 (paperback) | ISBN 9781640655171 (ebook)
Subjects: LCSH: Prayer--Christianity. | Children--Prayers and devotions.
Classification: LCC BV215 .G67 2022 (print) | LCC BV215 (ebook) | DDC 248.3/2--dc23/eng/20211118
LC record available at https://lccn.loc.gov/2021048218
LC ebook record available at https://lccn.loc.gov/2021048219

For Graham,
with love

May today there be peace within.

May you trust God that you are exactly where
you are meant to be.

May you not forget the infinite possibilities
that are born of faith.

May you use those gifts that you have received,
and pass on the love that has been given to you.

May you be content knowing you are a child of God.

Let this presence settle into your bones,
and allow your soul the freedom
to sing, dance, praise, and love.

It is there for each and every one of us.

—TERESA OF ÁVILA

Contents

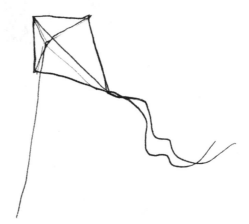

Introduction

A few days ago, my dog, Scarlett, and I met a dog named Ruby at the dog park. She and Scarlett started sniffing and circling each other, deciding whether they should become best friends. When Scarlett is at the dog park, it's like she's at her own birthday party, it's time to open a big stack of presents, and she can't decide which one to open first. Except in her case, it's choosing which dog to race around the park with her. We've met dozens of dogs over the years, but I won't forget Ruby. She has the most amazing eyes: one is brown, and one is a bright, icy blue.

What color are *your* eyes? Brown? Black? Green? Gray? Blue? Hazel? Are they two different colors, like Ruby's? Did you know that every person's iris, that colored part of the eye, is *completely unique*? No two people on earth have identical irises; our eyes are as unique as our fingerprints! And, like eyes and fingerprints, no two people in the world have the same voice—no one in the world sounds just like you do.

No one's eyes, fingerprints, or voice is just like yours . . . and no one prays exactly like you do either. Or feels the way you feel when you pray. Sometimes praying feels comfortable and easy, like taking a bath or petting a cat. Other times, it can feel clumsy and awkward, like when you trip on an uneven crack on the sidewalk. Praying can also feel as ordinary as filling up a glass with water.

More than a thousand years ago, a monk described prayer as the "raising of one's mind and heart to God or the requesting of good things from God."* Every person does

---

* *Catechism of the Catholic Church*, 2nd ed. (Vatican City: Libreria Editrice Vaticana, 2019), paragraph 2590.

this in their own way. Some people are perfectly motionless when they pray. Some sit in church on hard wooden benches. Others kneel. Some people close their eyes and fold their hands. Some people pray all by themselves; others pray in a roomful of other praying people. Often people use words to pray, either by reading what someone else has written or by saying whatever pops into their minds, like when you're talking with a friend. But we don't just *think* our prayers; we can move our bodies in prayer by dancing, walking, or even spinning in a chair. Some count along with their prayers, using beads on a string. Some sing their prayers, and some paint them. Some people just look at the clouds and let their thoughts and feelings float up into the sky. Others write down their prayers and slip them into a box or bowl. These are only a few of the ways people open their minds and hearts to God's presence.

monk: A monk is a member of a religious community of men who promise to obey God, live simply, and not get married.

That's another way to describe prayer: it's *being open to God*, as strange as that may sound. Part of this "being open" is knowing that God is a mystery, and that people have always used different names to describe God and different ways to talk to God.

Each chapter in this book includes a short prayer that uses names for God that we find in the Bible. You might have heard God called "Holy One" or "Creator" and you may pray to Jesus, but did you know that God is also called "Fount of Justice," "She Who Speaks Life," "Majesty of the Heavens," "Mother of Mountains," and "Wisdom" in the scriptures? This book will introduce new names to you that you can use when you are opening yourself to God, and it also describes many different ways to pray. As you read it, notice what ideas or names grab your attention. Try them out when you pray.

There are many ways to start prayers, but how can we *end* them? Many of us say "Amen." That word just means something like "So be it" or "This is what I really think." You can say "Amen" when you're done praying or you can just nod your head or shrug or say, "Okay, that's what I really feel" or "Over and out for now" or "Talk to you later!" You can choose to end your prayers in your own way.

Throughout the Bible, people always prayed in their own individual ways. Hagar and Hannah prayed with tears. Jesus drew prayers in the dust. David danced, Jacob wrestled, Samuel listened, and Habakkuk raged. People prayed in their homes, outside, alone, or in groups, and in places of worship. They prayed all through the day or night, whenever they had something to say. There's no right or wrong way to pray or right or wrong place to pray. There's no wrong way to start or end our prayers. Prayer is for everyone, and you can't make a mistake as you raise your mind and heart to the God who made you and who loves you for the wonderfully unique person you are.

CHAPTER 1

Sing

What was your favorite song when you were a little kid? "Baby Shark"? "Baby Bumblebee"? "The Wheels on the Bus"? (Maybe you still love those songs!) How do you feel when you hear the first few notes of one of your favorite songs? What song do you love best now? What do you like about it? The words? The beat? The melody? The way it rhymes? Maybe a song is your favorite because it reminds you of a happy time in your life or the person who first sang it to you.

Singing is fun, and it not only makes you feel good but actually keeps your brain and the rest of your body healthy! It's easier to memorize things when we sing them—chances are, you learned your ABCs by singing the alphabet song. Scientists say that our brains are made to remember patterns in music much better than when we just hear words spoken. They've also done lots of research that shows other positive effects of singing.

Gross as it might sound, our saliva—otherwise known as "spit"—reveals that, after a person sings, they are more relaxed. Singing also helps to keep people from getting sick by boosting the immune system.* When you sing with other people, your body releases chemicals called "endorphins" that lift your mood. Here's a funny fact too: researchers say that people who sing are less likely to have snoring problems!

---

* G. Kreutz, S. Bongard, S. Rohrmann, V. Hodapp, and D. Grebe, "Effects of Choir Singing or Listening on Secretory Immunoglobulin A, Cortisol, and Emotional State," *Journal of Behavioral Medicine* 27, no. 6 (December 2004): 623–35, https://pubmed.ncbi.nlm.nih.gov/15669447/.

Those are just a few good reasons to let
loose and SING!

(Baby shark, doo doo doo doo doo doo . . . !)

The word "sing" appears hundreds of
times in the Bible, and people are told or
commanded to sing many times too. "Sing to
the LORD a new song!" says Psalm 96:1;
"Sing praises to our King!" says Psalm 47:6.
Ephesians 5:19 (NIV): "Sing and make
music from your heart to the Lord!" And
Colossians 3:16 says we should sing to God
with "gratitude in [our] hearts."

Why do you think God likes singing so much?

Maybe it's because God knows singing is good for us and
makes us happy.

Maybe it's because God is a singer too. We read in the
Hebrew Bible that God sings over God's people (Zephaniah
3:17).

It was the apostle Paul who wrote the words above, about
singing with gratitude and from our hearts. And he practiced
what he preached. Paul sang not only when he was happy
but also on his very worst days. Even when he was put in
prison! Once, Paul and his friend Silas, who were traveling
and telling people about God's love, got into trouble. People
said they were "disturbing the peace." Paul and Silas were
beaten by the police and then locked away in prison.

That same night, around midnight, Paul and Silas were
praying and singing hymns to God when there was a strong
earthquake. It was so fierce that the foundation of the building shifted and the doors to all the prison cells were knocked

open. The earthquake woke the prison guard up, and when he saw that all the doors were open, he thought the prisoners had escaped. He thought he would lose his job—or worse—when his bosses found out what had happened. He felt desperate! But Paul shouted, "It's okay, we're all here!"

That night, the guard brought Paul and Silas home to his own house, got them cleaned up, bandaged their wounds, and gave them dinner. After that dramatic and unexpected night, the guard himself came to know that God loved him. He and his whole family came to know God.

I wonder if the prison scared Paul and Silas, and if singing made them feel braver in that place.

I wonder what songs Paul and Silas were singing?

I wonder whether the songs they sang that night became favorites of the guard, their new friend.

▨   ▨   ▨   ▨   ▨

TRY IT!

1. Put on your favorite song and sing it with your full voice. Let your song be a prayer of praise to our music-loving God.

2. The word "psalm" means "song," and the psalms we find in the Bible are poems that were written to be sung. In the book of Psalms, there are songs about anger, thankfulness, being lonely, joy . . . and many other things. No matter what you might be feeling, there is a psalm that can help you express yourself.

Read Psalm 104:33 (NIV):

I will sing to the LORD all my life; I will sing praise to my God as long as I live.

"Praise" means to celebrate or worship or honor something or someone.

Make a list of five things or people you are thankful for.

You could pray,

> I praise you, Almighty God, for:
>
> _____ (something in nature)
>
> _____ (someone you love)
>
> _____ (your favorite song)
> *Amen.*

3. Spirituals are songs that were created by African Americans from the time they were forced into slavery. They expressed their sadness and sang about the hardships they endured. They sang about stories of freedom and hope in the Bible, and they found courage and strength by singing these songs.

Read these lines from a famous African American spiritual "Ev'ry Time I Feel the Spirit":

> Ev'ry time I feel the Spirit moving in my heart
> I will pray.
> Ev'ry time I feel the Spirit moving in my heart
> I will pray.

What does God's spirit feel like when it's moving in your heart?

What songs might you sing when you are lonely or hurting?

What songs make you feel brave?

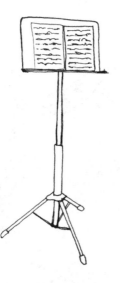

One Who Is,
Singing God,
Thank you for the gift
of music.
Amen.

CHAPTER 2
Touch

Look at one of your hands. Turn it over so your palm is facing up, and lightly trace the folds and creases you see there. Now look closely at your fingertips. The lines on the palm of your hand and the swirls and ridges of your fingerprints are unique to you. No one else's hands are just like yours.

And that's not the only amazing thing about your hands.

Did you know that the human hand has about a hundred thousand nerves, and each and every one of our fingertips has more than three thousand "touch receptors"? Also known as nerve endings or receptive fields, these help you recognize hot and cold, vibrations, tickling, and whether something is sharp or smooth or rough the very second you touch it. Those touch receptors are constantly talking to our brains, allowing us to feel and name everything from the cozy sensation of petting a cat to the tap-tap-tap of using a computer keyboard. They also prevent us from getting hurt. When you reach, for instance, for a cup of hot chocolate, if the mug's too hot, your touch receptors let you know (HOT! HOT!) and you pull your hand back and let it cool down before picking it up.

These receptors also help us get countless everyday things done easily. Reach for a pencil and your hand will get ready to pick it up by making a pinching motion with your fingers—without you even thinking about it. Or as you grab your water bottle or reach out to open a door, your hand turns on its side, ready to perform those simple tasks.

Some people say that touch is the most mysterious of our five senses.

Which of your senses—touch? taste? sight? smell? hearing?—do *you* think is the most special?

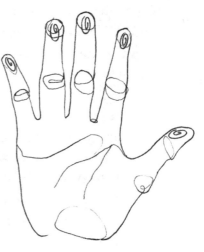

One of the ways Jesus prayed was with his hands.

Once, very early in the morning, Jesus was teaching people about God's love. Just then, some men interrupted him, bringing a woman along with them. They said she had been caught doing something bad. They were bullying her, and they wanted to embarrass and even hurt her. They wanted Jesus to tell them that she even deserved to *die* for the bad thing she had done.

But Jesus looked at the woman the way he looks at you; he saw her with eyes of love. After they told him what she'd done, Jesus was quiet and simply crouched down on the ground. Maybe he got down low to show the woman that he wasn't upset with her. Maybe it felt less scary to her to see him that way. Maybe it distracted the angry men when he did that and made them wonder what he was doing. Maybe being quiet and getting down on the ground gave him time to think.

Then, he drew in the dirt with his fingertips.

What do you think he drew?

I wonder if he might have been writing the word "love." Or maybe he was just drawing patterns in the dust, just to calm himself and everyone else down. Maybe he needed a moment to think about how to answer them.

When he stood up again, he asked the angry men if they'd ever done anything wrong. He asked if anyone there was perfectly perfect. His point was that *everyone* makes mistakes, *everyone* does things that they know are wrong sometimes. This made the men quiet down, and they left, one by one by one, without hurting the woman. They knew the truth about themselves: they had no right being unkind to that woman. They were just the same; no one is perfect. Jesus then gently told the woman that she could go. He gave her hope about what the rest of her life would be like. And then he continued teaching people about God's love.

Jesus knows the truth about us. He knows that we are weak sometimes, afraid sometimes, hurt sometimes. He doesn't want to judge or embarrass us. Instead, he looks at us with eyes of love and touches our hearts with a calming message of love, light, and freedom.

(You can read this story in John 8:1–11.)

TRY IT!

Here are a few ways to pray with your hands:

1. Open your hands and hold them in front of you, palms up. Imagine that you are opening yourself to God. Close your eyes and just sit quietly with your hands open.

2. Just as Jesus traced a prayer in the dust, you can trace a prayer with your fingers. Trace the labyrinth on this page as a prayer.

3. Make the sign of the cross over yourself with your fingertips. The sign of the cross is made by first touching your hand to your forehead, then down to your lower chest or stomach, and then to one shoulder and then the other.

4. Use American Sign Language to pray "Thank you, God" with your hands.

- To sign "Thank you," use your dominant hand (your dominant hand is your right hand if you are right-handed, your left hand if you are left-handed) and place your fingers near your lips, with your hand as flat as possible. Move your hand forward and slightly downward.

- To sign "God," swipe one of your hands in front of your head, your thumb touching your forehead, then pull it downward to your chest area.

Jesus,
Let my hands be hands of love.
Amen.

CHAPTER 3

Listen

Spell out the word "listen": L-I-S-T-E-N. Shuffle those letters around like a deck of cards, and you get another word: S-I-L-E-N-T. Being *silent* can help us to *listen* well but listening is not only about being quiet while someone else is talking. It's about staying focused on the other person. Listening well to others shows them that we respect them and that they are important to us. Doesn't it feel good when someone is really listening to you? When they don't interrupt or seem distracted? When they just focus on what you're trying to say? Friends really listen to each other.

We can be silent when we pray, too, and just sit, allowing God to speak to us. But it's not always easy to listen, especially in prayer. Life is pretty noisy. Even when you are quietly sitting still, you might hear sirens or rushing traffic outside, or the TV in the next room, or the neighbors walking around upstairs.

Listening is a skill that can be practiced. We can get better at it. One way to become a better listener is to practice what's called "whole body listening." Our ears, after all, aren't the only part of the body we use when we are listening. We use our *eyes* to look at the person who's speaking. Are they smil-

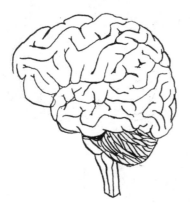

ing? Do they look nervous or upset? Are they using their hands to gesture or signal or sign? Are they jumpy or calm? We use our *brains* to understand what someone is saying, and we also use our *hearts* when we listen with kindness.

People listen well in different ways. Some people make noises when they are listening. Maybe they say "mmm-hmm" or make other sounds. Some people might fold their hands together or put them in their pockets. Others like keeping their hands busy when they're listening by fidgeting with something or flapping them around.

You know when someone is telling you a wonderful story, you find yourself leaning toward them, almost like you want their words to knock right up against you? Leaning toward the person who's speaking is another way to practice whole body listening.

When we keep our thoughts and attention right where we are, it's much easier for us to hear what someone is telling us, whether it's our teacher or friend or even our Creator God.

The name "Samuel" means "God has heard," and there is a story in the Bible about a time when a boy named Samuel heard God's actual voice. (That's a rare thing to happen!) The story began years before he was born when Samuel's mother, Hannah, went to the temple, like you might go to church, to pray. Hannah was very sad that day because she wanted to be a mother, but she couldn't become pregnant. She prayed silently, just moving her lips. Hannah wept as she begged God to give her a child.

Hannah's prayers *were* answered, and later she gave birth to Samuel. You can see why she gave him a name that means "God has heard." She felt grateful that God had heard her prayers asking for a child.

When Samuel was a young boy, Hannah brought him to the same temple where God had heard her. She wanted to give a gift of thanks to God. She decided that Samuel would live in the temple and serve God. A priest named Eli took care of Samuel when he was there. One night when Samuel was about twelve years old, he was lying in bed when he thought he heard Eli call for him. It was strange, to be sure, as the old man had never done that before.

He ran to Eli to ask what he wanted. Eli, awoken from deep sleep, told Samuel to go back to bed. He said he had *not* called out to Samuel. This happened a few more times that night, but each time Samuel ran to Eli's bedside, the priest told him he hadn't called his name and sleepily told the boy to go back to bed. Finally, Eli realized that it must be *God* calling Samuel's name, so he told the boy to go back to bed again, but he said if Samuel heard his name being called another time, he should answer God, saying, "Speak, for your servant is listening!"

Samuel went back to bed and, sure enough, God called out to him again, saying, "Samuel! Samuel!"

Samuel said, "Speak, for your servant is listening!" and God spoke to him, giving him a message for Eli.

(You can read this story in 1 Samuel 3:1–15.)

I wonder whether Eli was angry or irritated at Samuel
that night for waking him up.

I wonder how Samuel felt when he realized it wasn't Eli,
but God who was calling his name.

What might it sound like if God said your name aloud?

What message might God have for you?

■ ■ ■ ■ ■

TRY IT!

1. Pray in silence, and practice listening for God's voice.

- Turn off your phone, TV, music . . . just be as silent as
  possible.

- Set a timer for one minute and sit still, doing nothing
  at all.

- Breathe in through your nose slowly and then quietly
  exhale through your mouth; do this three times.

- Let your shoulders relax and close your eyes until the
  timer sounds.

- Invite God to speak to you by saying, "I am here. I am
  listening."

2. Go on a sound treasure hunt.

- Grab a notebook or piece of paper and sit down in one place. It could be inside your home or school, or outside at a park.

- Listen!

- Write down every single sound you hear, from the softest creak in the floorboards or chirp of a bird to the loudest siren or radio.

- Does the pencil or pen, as you write down what you hear, make a tiny sound too?

> God Who Speaks,
> Here I am.
> I'm listening.
> *Amen.*

CHAPTER 4

Create

An "icon" is a religious work of art that is sometimes called a "window into heaven." When the artist is creating it, they are thinking about the Bible and praying. Most of the time, icons show Jesus; his mother, Mary; saints; or angels, and they are painted on pieces of wood. Sometimes they are carved in stone or formed with metal or clay. But however they are made, people often say they were "written" (not carved or painted) because each stroke of the artist's brush or shaping of the clay is understood as a prayer.

There are other interesting things about icons. Often when you see one, you'll know it's an icon because the people look a little . . . well . . . different. In icons, people's foreheads are taller than they are in real life because the person "writing" the icon wants to show that Jesus, Mary, and other holy people are wiser than regular people. Making their foreheads look bigger is meant to show that their

brains are bigger. Most of the time, too, people in icons have their mouths closed. This is to signal to someone seeing the icon that silence before God is a good thing.

⬛ ⬛ ⬛ ⬛ ⬛

In one famous icon of Jesus, he's shown to have two very differently shaped eyes. One is larger, one is smaller. One eye is beautiful, and one looks a little swollen like he's been hit in the face or got stung by a bee. There is definitely something wrong with it!

In the book of Isaiah, in the Hebrew Bible, the promised Messiah is described as someone who's sad, who is not popular or good-looking. It says he is the kind of person that people don't want to look at or see . . . like the kind of person that makes you want to cross over to the other side of the street when you see them (Isaiah 53:1–3). Maybe the writer of that icon had read the verse in Isaiah that says that the coming Messiah would have "no beauty" and would be "rejected" and wanted to show that. Maybe the icon writer wrote those two very different eyes—one nice-looking and one not—to say that Jesus was both God and human, both perfect Divinity and regular person, at the same time.

Messiah: The Hebrew word *Mashiach*, or "Messiah," means "the one anointed with oil" and in the Hebrew Bible, the Messiah is the future deliverer of the Jewish people. Christians believe that Jesus was the Messiah.

I wonder how I can remember to look at others the way God looks at me, with kindness and curiosity.

I wonder if reminding myself that we are all beloved children of God will help me open my heart to others.

Why do you think the icon writer made one eye perfect and the other eye different?

How would you feel if you saw a person in real life who had eyes like that, one looking swollen and the other perfect?

What is one way you could look at someone, even someone who is different from you, with love?

TRY IT!

Here are some ways to pray with icons or other works of art:

1. Look at the icon in this chapter. What is the first thing you notice about it? What parts do you like? What parts make you want to look away? Make a copy of the icon and color it in. Because some people think icons are holy and special, some people kiss icons. If you would like, kiss the back of your hand, and then touch it to the icon after you finish coloring it in.

2. Create a letter to the Divine by making your own icon.
You can use words or colors or clay or fabric or whatever you like. It could be a note, a painting, a sculpture,
or loops and doodles with a pencil. Let your prayer flow
from you with every movement of your hand.

Thank you, Creator God,
for the windows into heaven
that I see around me.
Help me to see others with eyes of love.
Amen.

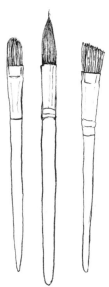

CHAPTER 5
Laugh

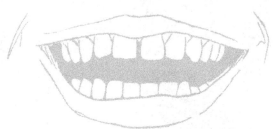

There's an old saying that "laughter is the best medicine." Have you ever heard that? It's actually based on a verse in the Bible, Proverbs 17:22, that reads, "A cheerful heart is a good medicine."

Although it's an old-fashioned thing to say—maybe something your grandparents or even *their* parents said— there's a lot of scientific proof that laughter, in fact, really is amazing for our health. When we laugh, for instance, feel-good chemicals called "endorphins" are released in our bodies. Also, laughing makes our hearts beat faster, and this is important because this helps our bodies move oxygen and blood to our muscles better and can help prevent heart disease. Our immune systems are also boosted when we laugh, helping us to stay safe from viruses or other things that could make us sick. Laughing makes us feel less stressed, happier, and more relaxed. So maybe it really *is* the best medicine!

What makes *you* laugh?

Some people like to be tickled. (Of course, others absolutely do *not*!)

Other people find certain words funny, words like "borborygmus" or "bumbershoot" or "cattywampus" or "doodlesack"!

borborygmus: The sound of your "stomach" rumbling or gurgling. (It's caused by fluids or gas moving around in your intestines.)

bumbershoot: Umbrella.

cattywampus: Something that's not lined up correctly and a little off-center, like a bookshelf with books sloppily stacked there, some with their spines out, some backward.

doodlesack: Bagpipes.

Some people love jokes, like:

What do you call a duck
on the Fourth of July?
A fire quacker!

How do you make a hot dog stand?
Take away its chair!

Why did the boy eat his homework?
Because his teacher told him it was a piece of cake!

Some situations make us laugh, especially strange, unexpected, or unlikely ones—like a dog wearing a wig or a cat with glasses on. Exaggeration, stretching the truth, or making things seem much bigger than they are is funny too, like: "That taxi was going a hundred thousand miles an hour!" or "I could eat an entire mountain of pancakes!"

What makes you laugh?
  Something you hear?
  Something you see?
  When is the last time you laughed really hard?

The Bible doesn't tell us much about what Jesus was like as a child. We know he had a lot of younger siblings and that his father was a carpenter. He probably helped with his younger brothers and sisters, and we know that Joseph taught him how to build things. Because Jesus was fully human, we know he laughed and played and learned and did many other things just like you do.

We also know that when he was twelve years old Jesus got into really big trouble with his parents. Every year, his family celebrated the holidays in the city of Jerusalem, more than sixty miles from their hometown of Nazareth. As they were headed home that year, Jesus slipped away from his parents and returned to the big city. Maybe their family was traveling with a big group of friends, aunts, uncles, and cousins, so it wasn't until Mary and Joseph were nearly home to Nazareth that they realized Jesus was missing. Mary and Joseph were, of course, very worried. They finally found him, days later, back in the temple in Jerusalem. Jesus was teaching the adults there, and everyone said they were shocked by how smart he was and how much he understood about God.

Jesus, of course, did a lot of public speaking over the course of his life. And everybody knows, most great teachers and speakers have great senses of humor.

So . . . was Jesus funny? Although none of the Gospels include knock-knock jokes or examples of Jesus using silly words to make people laugh, they do show a Jesus who had a good sense of humor. He often told funny stories when he was teaching people about God and about how to treat others with love. He seemed most fond of exaggerating.

Jesus taught that we should love God and others . . . and not love money. One time he told a strange and funny story to explain this, saying, "It is easier for a camel to go through the eye of a needle than for someone who is rich to enter the kingdom of God" (Mark 10:25). The "eye" of a needle is that tiny hole where the end of a piece thread goes. How in the world could a camel (and what a hilarious animal to bring to mind!) get through that tiny hole?

Another unexpected story Jesus told was about someone who was judging (meaning looking down on or thinking unkind thoughts about) someone else. He said, "Why do you look at the speck of sawdust in your brother's eye and pay no attention to the plank in your own eye?" (Matthew 7:3–4, NIV) A plank is a big piece of wood. So, if you imagine this scene, a person with a huge piece of wood sticking out of their face is finding fault with someone else because they have a tiny little speck of sawdust in their eye. It's ridiculous! And judging other people is silly, too, Jesus shows us. We all have problems and weaknesses and faults. Instead of pointing out these things in other people, we can humbly be aware that, like us, they aren't perfect. We can look at others with kindness and a light heart.

TRY IT!

1. Write your own "knock-knock" prayer. Here are some knock-knock jokes to give you ideas:

> *Knock knock!*
> Who's there?
> *Nobel.*
> Nobel who?
> *Nobel . . . that's why I knocked!*

> *Knock knock!*
> Who's there?
> *Tank.*
> Tank who?
> *You're welcome!*

Maybe one knock-knock prayer could be:
> *Knock knock, God!*
> Who's there?
> *It's me right now!*
> It's me right now who?
> *It's me right now who is thanking you!*
> *Amen.*

2. Cheer someone up with humor. Think of someone in your life who seems like they could use a little cheering up. Try to lift their mood by:

- mailing them a handwritten note
- drawing them a funny picture
- telling them your favorite joke
- bringing them a treat

Bright Morning Star,
Thank you for the gift of laughter.
Open my heart
to the joy around me!
Amen.

CHAPTER 6
Question

Have you ever thought—or shouted—the words "Why?" or "It's not fair!"?

Maybe it was when you were younger and your parent said it was time to leave the park or playground, but it felt like you'd just gotten there. Or when you've been in trouble for something you didn't even do. Or when something important got canceled or something you cared about got ruined or broken.

You might also have furiously said, "It's not fair!" about situations even more serious than whether you got what you wanted. Maybe you think those words when you see an upsetting news headline. You wonder why God allows hurricanes or why there are people who get murdered because of the color of their skin or why there are refugees.

Why, God, why?

It's just not fair!

When you feel those words, "It's not fair!" rising in your mind and heart, it's often because you are looking at something you can't control.

You might feel powerless, weak, and frustrated—all at the same time—in those moments.

You might feel *furious* toward God and wonder why God doesn't make things right, put good people in power, protect people from violence.

You can ask God about all of this, and you won't be the first person to do so.

▪ ▪ ▪ ▪ ▪

Hundreds of years before Jesus was born, a prophet named Habakkuk asked God about the violence, injustice, and suffering he witnessed. We don't know a lot about Habakkuk, but we do know that he was a prophet who worked at the temple. Prophets were people who had special wisdom. God chose prophets to speak words of comfort to people and to let them know when they were moving off track and failing to live and love well. We also know that throughout the book of the Bible that is named for him, Habakkuk *demanded* that God answer him about the sad state of the world. Habakkuk was different than other prophets; other ones simply spoke the messages that God gave them to share but Habakkuk pushed back against God when he thought something wasn't fair.

"How long, LORD," Habakkuk prayed, "must I call for help, but you do not listen?" (Habakkuk 1:2, NIV).

Later he asked, "Why do you tolerate wrongdoing? Destruction and violence are before me; there is strife and conflict abounds . . . the law is powerless, and justice never goes forth."

Why wasn't God making things better?

Habakkuk believed in the Almighty, and he told God that it wasn't fair the way things were going in the world.

"It's just not fair!"

John Lennon, who was a musician and peace activist and someone you might have heard of from the band the Beatles, said: "Everything will be okay in the end. If it's not okay, it's not the end."

This is the way Habakkuk's prayer was answered: God said, "It's not the end."

Habakkuk understood that God is a mystery and was doing something that he couldn't understand. Habakkuk decided to trust in the goodness of God and that God, in God's own time, was working things out.

TRY IT!

1. Read this blessing:*

May God bless you
by making you feel angry
when things are not fair and
sad when you see people hurting.
May God give you friends
who tell the truth
about you, about themselves, and about the world.
May you and your friends be world-changers
who do good and make peace.
Amen.

In what way might tears be a blessing? Or anger at injustice a blessing?

How might you make a difference in the world, instead of waiting for God to come to the rescue?

2. Write a list of a few things that seem wrong in the world. These could be things like poverty, hunger, homelessness, or sickness. Now, with a trusted adult, think of at least one thing you could do to make things more right and fair. Could you bring food to a food pantry? Could you give money to a place that helps people experiencing homelessness?

---

* Adapted from "A Fourfold Franciscan Blessing," written by Sister Ruth Marlene Fox, https://www.gingerling.co.uk/the-origin-of-a-franciscan-prayer-a-non-traditional-blessing/.

Mysterious God—
I wonder, "Why?"
I feel like "it's not fair!"
I watch and wait
for you to make things right
in the world.
Show me what is true
and how I can make things better here.
Amen.

CHAPTER 7
Count

All over the world and all throughout history, people have opened their hearts and raised their voices in prayer to the mystery we call God. People of all faiths pray silent prayers, use written prayers, sing their prayers, and pray with other believers. Muslims pray to  Allah five times a day—at dawn, after midday, afternoon, after sunset, and at night. Devout Hindus pray at least twice a day, at dawn and at dusk. Observant Jews silently recite the *Amidah*, or Standing Prayer, three times every weekday. While Christians in religious life—people like monks and nuns—often follow a schedule in their daily and nightly prayers, other Christian believers do not. Some Christians pray first thing in the morning, others say grace before meals, some say their prayers right before they go to sleep, and others pray only when they're in church—or when they are having a hard time.

People of many faiths, including Buddhists, use prayer beads, called *malas*, to keep track of how many and what prayers, or *mantras*, they've said. Catholic prayer beads, called rosaries, have fifty-nine beads as well as a crucifix, or cross, and a medal. When they pray the rosary, Catholics say very specific prayers while touching the different parts of the strand of beads. One of the sets of prayers is the "Hail Mary," and there are ten beads where this prayer is repeated ten times, all in a row.

It is:

Hail Mary, full of grace,
the Lord is with you.
Blessed are you among women,
and blessed is the fruit of your womb, Jesus.
Holy Mary, Mother of God,
pray for us sinners,
now and at the hour of our death.
Amen.

mantra: Originally used in Buddhism and Hinduism, a mantra is a "sacred utterance," a word or phrase that those who speak them believe have spiritual power.

sinner: A sinner is someone who sins. The Bible tells us that everyone is a sinner (Romans 3:23). When we sin, it's often because of a choice we've made that hurts us or hurts other people. The good news is that God has already made things right for us and forgives us, even before we ask!

Rosary beads are a version of what desert fathers and mothers—hermits and devout followers of Jesus—used for prayer not long after Jesus's death and resurrection. They created knotted prayer ropes, using the knots to keep track of how many times they said the Jesus Prayer.

The Jesus Prayer is:

"Lord Jesus Christ, Son of God, have mercy on me, a sinner."

When a prayer like the Hail Mary or the Jesus Prayer is repeated over and over, it can help the person praying to calm down and can make them feel closer to God. But you don't have to say these words if you notice they don't fit for you. Any words said in prayer can become your mantra. These words could be "Jesus loves me" or "It is well with my soul" or "May everyone be happy." (Or choose any words that are special to you!) The apostle Paul directed believers to pray the way they breathe—without pausing or counting how many times they speak the words. He wrote, "Pray without ceasing, give thanks in all circumstances; for this is the will of God in Christ Jesus for you" (1 Thessalonians 5:17–18).

It's interesting, when you are getting to know someone, to learn what it is that they keep count of in their own life. Maybe they can tell you, without even blinking, how many stuffed animals they own. Or how old they were when they moved from one house to their new one. Or how many stops on the train it is from their home to their school.

People are good at keeping track.

One thing Jesus warned us about keeping track of is how many times someone else has hurt our feelings or otherwise wronged us.

Once, Jesus's friend Peter asked Jesus a question about keeping track. He asked how often he needed to forgive another person.

"How often should I forgive?" Peter asked. "As many as seven times?" (Matthew 18:21–22).

Seven *is* a lot, don't you think?

If someone hurt your feelings seven times in a row, and you forgave them the first six times, wouldn't it be a little hard to accept their apology that seventh time? You'd probably wonder: so, what's to say they won't just do it *again*?

You might think Jesus would say, "Well, Peter. You've forgiven your friend so many times. That's super nice! Seven times is just fine. If that person hurts you an eighth time, there's no need to forgive. You've done enough."

But, as usual, Jesus surprises us.

In some translations of the Bible, Jesus tells Peter he should forgive other people 490 times! In others, it's 77 times. Either way, seven times is not nearly enough. But maybe it's not about keeping track or counting how many times we forgive someone else. Maybe it's about being generous with other people . . . and with ourselves. There's an old saying that when we forgive someone it's like letting someone out of jail, but the person who gets to be free is ourselves. Forgiveness sets us free!

Maybe Jesus asks us not to keep track of how many times we forgive because he wants us to live fully and freely . . . and unforgiveness keeps us from doing that.

■ ▪ ▪ ▪ ▪

TRY IT!

Here are some ways to count out your prayers:

1. Count your blessings. Get out a piece of paper and number it 1–10. See if you can list ten things that make you happy. If that's too easy, make it twenty or thirty or even a hundred things! At the bottom of the page, you could write: "Thank you, God!" You could also use ten beads to make your own strand of prayer beads and, as you touch each one, say the name of someone you love or a problem you're worried about.

2. Bounce a basketball. Bounce it over and over. Every time the ball hits the pavement or sidewalk, say (out loud or silently) the name of someone you care about or someone you are willing to forgive. You can repeat the same name, over and over.

3. Tap out a "five finger prayer." Tapping on this book or a table or even on your arm, tap your thumb, then index finger, then third . . . all the way to your pinky, saying one word with each tap.

You can pray any five words that mean something to you.

Here are a few to try:

- Thank
- You
- For
- Your
- Love

-

- Help
- Me
- To
- Forgive
- Others

or write and tap your own five finger prayer:

1 _____

2 _____

3 _____

4 _____

5 _____

Merciful God,
Watch over me now,
and help me
to forgive myself
and others
without ever counting
or keeping track.
Amen..

CHAPTER 8
Petition

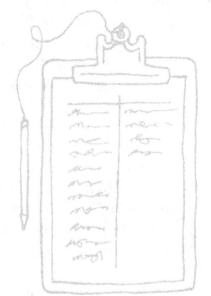

Have you ever heard of—or even signed—a petition?

When we want to make a positive change in our community, we can write or sign petitions about things that matter to us. For example, if you want to fight climate change and global warming, you could *petition* your school to plant more trees or to invest in recycling bins for the cafeteria.

A strong petition clearly names the problem and how it's affecting people. ("The climate is in crisis and kids at our school are throwing away aluminum cans instead of recycling them.") It then may paint a positive picture of the solution. ("Aluminum cans return from the recycling bin to the store over

petition: A request to change something.

and over, and do not need to become trash.") It usually ends by making a simple request. ("Please put recycling bins in our lunchroom so our soda cans can be reused.")

When we petition in our prayers, we ask for God's help either for ourselves or for others. You might need help letting go of uneasy or fearful feelings after a nightmare or an argument or another unpleasant experience. Or you might petition God on behalf of someone else, asking for their healing from illness or from hurt feelings. Your prayer of petition might be very short; you might see an ambulance passing by and say a short word on behalf of whoever is inside. ("Be with them, God," you might say, petitioning God for a good outcome for that stranger.)

In Matthew 18:19–20, Jesus says that when even a few people are praying together, he himself is with them. We can pray with our families or friends for the needs of others, and God will truly be with us as we pray. Our prayers might not be answered right away or in a way that we can understand, but God is with us.

■ ■ ■ ■ ■

The book of Ruth is one of the shortest books of the Bible, but there are many things that make it important. One is that it is packed full of prayers and blessings. It also shows how things can seem really awful, but that things can get better. And its description of the love that can grow and deepen in our families is beautiful. Ruth isn't the only character in the story; Naomi, her mother-in-law, is also a major part of the book. And these women were people of prayer.

Naomi, we learn in the book of Ruth, had a very hard life. She had to leave her home because her country had a terrible famine. In times of famine—sometimes the result of extreme heat and not enough rain—people can't grow the food they need. Without enough food and water, people die of starvation. Famines still happen. Today, in countries including Nigeria, Somalia, and Yemen, millions of people face famine conditions.

famine: When large numbers of people can't get enough food for a long time. Famines can be caused by natural disasters like earthquakes and floods or by human factors such as wars.

After moving to a foreign country in order to escape the famine, Naomi's husband died. A few years later, both of her adult children, sons, also died. We don't know why they died. Perhaps their bodies were weak and sick after not having enough to eat for so long.

Naomi worked hard to survive, and she looked after her two daughters-in-law. When faced with loneliness, poverty, and sorrow, Naomi prayed. But she didn't just pray for herself. She prayed prayers of petition on behalf of her two daughters-in-law, asking God to be kind to them, that they would find rest, and that they would marry again (Ruth 1:8–9). Naomi and one of her daughters-in-law, Ruth, became extremely close friends. Ruth loved Naomi with her whole heart, and she prayed for her. Ruth asked God to keep them close and to take care of her mother-in-law.

God heard their prayers; Ruth and Naomi end up living in a good place with all their needs met. Ruth married again and kept Naomi close as she began a new life. The book ends with Naomi cradling her new grandson, Ruth's baby boy, her heart full of love and praise.

* * *

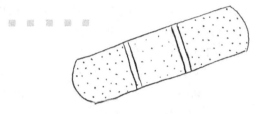

TRY IT!

1. Petition God on behalf of
people who are sick or suffering by making a healing board. Attach Band-Aids to a piece of poster board or paper and then write a name on each one. Or fill in the blank bandages on this page with the names of people

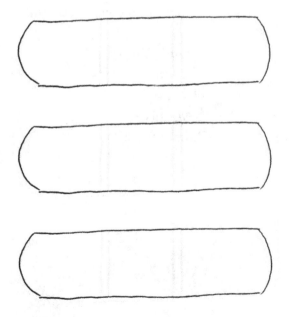

in need. Remember that God's healing can sometimes look like recovering, but it also can feel like comfort, even when you are sick. Not everyone gets better when we pray for them, but we know that God is always with us.

2. Pray for someone who is hurting or sad by putting your hand gently on their arm (ask their permission before touching them) or, if you aren't with that person, you could put your hand on their name or on a picture of them and imagine God's healing energy moving through you into them.

3. Pray a prayer of petition for someone or something you love:

   • Clearly describe the problem they are facing.

   • Imagine what a good outcome would look like.

   • Directly ask God to help that person or cause.

Lord of Justice,
I petition you:
Please bring change
to this world.
Take away sadness,
bring peace and joy.
Amen.

CHAPTER 9
See

You might hear people share their pronouns with others when they first meet. (They might say, for instance, "I'm Sal, and I use 'he/him.'") A pronoun is a word you can use instead of repeating someone's name over and over. For example, we don't say, "Ariana needed to get ready for school so Ariana took a shower and Ariana brushed Ariana's hair." Nah . . . that would be too many Arianas! Isn't it easier to say, "Ariana needed to get ready for school so *she* took a shower, and *she* brushed *her* hair"? (Ariana's pronouns are "she/her.")

"She" and "her" are pronouns, and others are "he," "him," "they," "them," and there are even more. Pronouns are important; when we use the pronouns that someone is most comfortable with, we're calling them by their right name. We're showing them respect and kindness. The way we talk about a person is important, and it affects the way we treat each other.

When we refer to things in the natural world (like trees, animals, and flowers), the pronoun most people use is "it."

"Look at that bird!" we might say. "It is building a nest up in that tree."

But not all people use "it" or "its" as a pronoun for things in nature. Some people use the pronouns "ki" and "kin."

Robin Wall Kimmerer is an Indigenous American author and college professor who hopes that *all* people will begin to use these pronouns for living things instead of "it." She thinks if we do, we'll show more respect and kindness to the earth. We'll feel more of a kinship—linked or related to—with other living things.

indigenous people: The first people who lived in a place. Other ways to describe Indigenous people are to use terms like "native people" or "First Nations people."

Kimmerer is a member of the Citizen Potawatomi Nation. She invites us to adopt the Native American idea of not thinking of parts of nature as cold objects that we just look at or use, but as *beings*. When we use the pronoun "it," we're talking about something that doesn't much matter, something that has no feelings or importance or life. A pair of scissors is an "it"; you use *it* to cut things. A fork is an "it"; you eat with *it*, and then you toss *it* in the sink or dishwasher.

Kimmerer says that when we speak about the land or trees or deer as if they were just things, we miss how much beauty they add to the world and how connected we are to them. Bees and horses and maple trees have lives, like we do. They create and communicate, like we do. Kimmerer asks us to save the pronoun "it" for "paperclips and bulldozers," but to use "ki" and "kin" when we are referring to "beings of Earth" in the living world.

If you want to try this out, the way we'd speak this way would be to say:

> "Look at that bird! Ki is building a nest up in
> that tree."

Or, if you were speaking about more than one thing, you could say,

> "The trees in this forest are so tall. Kin are so
> beautiful!"

What do you think a tree's preferred pronouns might be? A bird's? A butterfly's?

How might thinking about our kinship with other living things change the way we see or take care of the natural world?

Psalm 77:16 says,

When the waters saw you, they were afraid; the very deep trembled.

Can you imagine the ocean being afraid?
What would frighten the depths of the sea?

Psalm 19:1-2 (CEB) states:

Heaven is declaring God's glory;
    the sky is proclaiming his handiwork.
One day gushes the news to the next,
    and one night informs another what needs to
    be known.

How does the sky talk?

How do clouds make announcements?

I wonder how nature "pours forth speech." (That almost
    sounds to me like the natural world is a chatterbox!)
    I wonder whether nature prays.

Imagine seeing a flower blooming. I wonder if that is
    a prayer.

Might thunder and lightning be the sky praising God?

I wonder, too, if the ocean is praying when waves crash
    against a rocky coast.

TRY IT!

1. Go outside and sit in a park or beside a patch of grass. Look at a blade of grass, a tree, a bird and practice the "ki/kin" pronouns. Thank God for making a wonderful, living world.

2. Plant a seed and carefully nurture ki. See how ki sprouts and grows. Let your care of this plant be a prayer.

> She Who Speaks Life,
> Thank you for our living earth,
> help us to learn from
> and live well with
> trees and animals and land.
> Let us love kin better.
> *Amen.*

CHAPTER 10
Wrestle

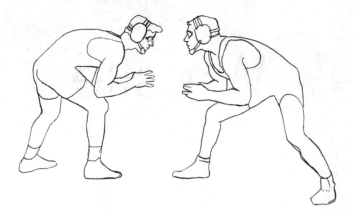

Have you ever watched a wrestling match on TV or in a school gym? Wrestlers struggle to stay on their feet and work hard to force their opponent to the ground. When a match ends, wrestlers are sweaty and tired out. Maybe sometimes you wrestle with your siblings until you're out of breath and laughing, just like wrestlers on the mat. The key to wrestling—whether in sport or when you're just goofing around—is hanging on tight and never letting go.

But what does this have to do with *prayer*?

Sometimes our feelings about God are confusing. Maybe you've asked God to make something better, but then you *still* got a bad grade on your test, or your broken arm *still* hurts, or your parents *still* got divorced.

You raised your mind and heart to God and trusted that your prayer would be answered . . . but it just feels like God isn't listening. You didn't see anything change, and you feel disappointed, frustrated, and maybe even really angry.

That's okay—prayer isn't all just "Thank you" or "Help me!"

We can offer *all* our feelings to God, even tangled and painful and angry ones.

In the very first book of the Bible, Genesis, we meet twin brothers who did *not* get along. Jacob and Esau were their names, and they not only *physically* wrestled with each other (and not in the fun way), but also struggled to be the favorite son in the family. Things only got worse when they grew up. When Jacob was an adult, he wanted God to protect him from Esau—he actually thought his brother was going to *murder* him. And Jacob was terrified.

Then, one night, when Jacob was trying to sleep, a stranger jumped on him. The two wrestled until the sun came up and it was morning. But it wasn't Esau but God who wrestled with Jacob, all night long. As exhausted as he was, Jacob never let go until God promised to protect and bless him. When the wrestling match ended, God did bless him. God also gave Jacob, which means "grabber," a new name. God named him "Israel." His new name means "struggles with God" or "one who sees God." One of the ways that God blessed Jacob was that the very day after their wrestling match, God brought Esau and Jacob together. They made up and lived the rest of their lives as loving brothers. What a happy ending to that tricky story!

(You can read this story in Genesis 32:22–30.)

Why do you think God wrestled with Jacob?

Do you ever wake up from a dream and wonder if it really happened?

What feelings about God do you wrestle with?

There are examples all through the Bible of people who wrestled in their prayers. They've said things like, "How long, LORD, have I called for help, And You do not hear?" (Habakkuk 1:2, NASB). Both David and even Jesus prayed when they felt abandoned and upset with God, asking: "Why have you forsaken me?" (Psalm 22:1 and Matthew 27:46). When you feel alone, disappointed, and have painful or difficult thoughts, follow Jesus's example, and tell God exactly what you're feeling.

compassionate: Caring about someone else and what they are feeling.

▦ ▦ ▦ ▦ ▦

TRY IT!

1. In yoga, the "easy pose" is a comfortable, cross-legged pose. Practicing this pose can calm us down when we feel stressed out. We can sit in easy pose when we pray.

- Sit down on the floor and stretch your legs out in front of you.

- Sit up straight, and then cross your legs—with your knees wide, tuck each foot under the opposite knee.

- Place your hands on your knees, palms down.

- Close your eyes, and take a few deep breaths, in through the nose and out through the mouth. Let your body relax and be still.

- After a minute or two, open your eyes and stretch your legs out straight in front of you again.

If you cannot sit cross-legged on the floor, sit up
straight in your chair, and rest your hands on your
knees, palms down. Close your eyes, and take a few
deep breaths, in through the nose and out through the
mouth. Let your body relax and be still.

yoga: A prayer practice from the Hindu religion that people of many
faiths (and no faith) use to pray, stretch, and experience calmness.
Yoga focuses on mindful breathing, exercise, and meditation.

2. Find an extra shoelace or a piece of cord, and tie knots
in it. Pull them tight, and then work to untangle them.
Imagine that these knots are your worries or unhappy
feelings and that God is smoothing them out for you.

Compassionate God,
Sometimes my feelings are tangled up in knots,
and I'm not even sure if you are there
or if you hear me when I pray.
But I believe you care about the
ups and downs in my life.
I ask that you bless me,
even when I feel like I'm wrestling with you.
Amen.

CHAPTER 11

Imagine

Have you heard of Ignatius of Loyola?

Born more than five hundred years ago into a large family, the boy "Iñigo" grew up and then spent the first part of his adult life as a knight in the Spanish military. In a battle against the French, he was hit in the legs with a cannonball and nearly died. During his recovery, he had to stay in bed for months. He spent that downtime reading the only books that were on hand: one was about Jesus and the other was about Christian saints. These books changed the course of his life, and he decided to leave the military and to spend most of his time in prayer. Later, he wrote a book of his own called *The Spiritual Exercises*.

He also founded the Society of Jesus, also known as the "Jesuits," a religious community in the Roman Catholic Church. Later, it was reported that Ignatius had performed miracles, and for this reason and for starting the Jesuit community, he was declared a saint by the church. Today, there are more than sixteen thousand Jesuit "brothers" (all Jesuits are men), and they work on behalf of global justice and peace. They also help others "discern God's presence in their lives," which is a fancy way of saying that they spend time with people and try to show people all the ways that God is being kind to them or helping them to become wiser.

saint: A person thought to be especially close to God, whose life and work help others follow Jesus.

In *The Spiritual Exercises*, Ignatius describes a way to pray by using our imagination. He believed that God speaks to us as through our thoughts, memories, and imaginations.

Think of a time when God spoke to you through your memories or your imagination. What was that like?

*What or who do you imagine when you picture yourself in the
presence of God?*

What makes you feel creative or imaginative?

What kind of things do you like to daydream about?

※ ※ ※ ※ ※

The story of Jesus feeding five
thousand people—with just a
little bread and a few fish—is
the only miracle that Jesus performed that is written about in
all the Gospels, or the four books
of the Bible that tell the story of
Jesus's life. In it, a huge crowd of
people were coming toward Jesus,
wanting to hear his teaching. Jesus asked one of his disci-
ples if there was a nearby marketplace where they could
buy bread to feed them.

His disciple, Philip, seemed irritated by Jesus's question.
He said, "It would take more than half a year's wages to buy
enough bread for each one to have a bite!" Jesus's disciples
had little, if any, money. Philip might have felt annoyed
that Jesus didn't seem to be aware of that.

Another disciple, Andrew, tried to brainstorm a solution
to their problem of having no money, no food, and a whole
lot of hungry people. He pointed out a boy who had a bit
of food and suggested that they share the boy's meal with
the crowd. The way the story is told, the boy likely offered
what he had.

Jesus accepted this offering, prayed, and then passed around the food.

You might know the rest of the story: not only did every single person eat as much as they wanted, but there were baskets and baskets of leftovers to be collected when everyone had finished.

The people were astonished, and they realized that God was with them that day.

(You can read this story in John 6:1–13.)

■　■　■　■　■

TRY IT!

Practice imaginative prayer with the story of Jesus feeding the five thousand.

Paint a picture in your mind of what it was like to be there that day. Imagine what the weather is like: Is it sunny? Gray and cloudy? Maybe it was even raining. Imagine people of all ages gathered around Jesus, some sitting alone and others chatting and laughing with family or friends. Picture babies, sleeping in their parents' arms or lying on a blanket in the grass or even crying. What sounds do you hear?

Keep creating a picture of that day, using all your senses:

1. What do you see?

2. What do you hear?

3. What do you smell?

4. What do you taste?

5. What do you feel?

Put yourself in the place of one of the characters in the story.

If you could be anyone in the story, who would you choose to be?

What would it feel like to be the child who shared their food?

As a bystander waiting for the meal, how do you feel?

What words of prayer does Jesus speak before he passes out the food?

What does the bread taste like? Is it thin like a cracker, or thick like a dinner roll?

What do you see in your imagination?

I wonder if anyone there that day thought Jesus was doing some kind of trick or was hiding baskets of food, maybe just over the other side of the hill.

I wonder whether Philip rolls his eyes when Jesus asks where they can buy bread.

I wonder if the boy feels proud when he sees thousands of people eating because he shared.

I wonder what Philip is thinking when he sees all that food!

> *What about Andrew?*
> *What about Jesus?*

You can try this practice with other Bible stories too. Put yourself into the scene, and really try to feel what the people might have been feeling.

The boy with the bread and fish reminds us that small gifts can do big things. What might you have that Jesus can use to help others?

Source of Life,
Thank you for the gift of imagination.
Keep me curious.
Feed my imagination!
Amen.

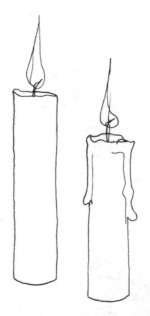

CHAPTER 12
Trust

Have you ever seen a toddler stand at the side of a swimming pool and jump right into their parent's outstretched arms? Maybe you've even done that yourself! Sometimes adults do something that is similar, called a "trust fall." Standing in a small crowd of people, they cross their arms over their chest, close their eyes, and let their body fall backward. The "spotters," or other people around them, catch them to keep them from falling to the ground. Sometimes trust falls are just for fun and sometimes they are done as team-building exercises for people who work together. Sometimes even rock stars do them, falling backward off the concert stage into a huge crowd of fans on the floor below them. The person doing the fall is, of course, confident that everyone will protect them and wants what's best for them. You only jump into someone's arms or do a trust fall when you are absolutely sure you'll be safely caught!

There are less dramatic ways, of course, of how people—and animals too—show us they trust us. When dogs look at us right in the eyes, it's a sign they trust us. And when cats rub against our legs, hoping we'll pet them, they're also expressing trust. When someone tells us they love us or tells us about something that embarrasses them or confuses them, they are trusting us to listen with kindness. Trust has to do with knowing the other person wants what is best for us. We trust each other when we know someone is on our side.

░ ░ ░ ░ ░

There are many stories of people trusting Jesus in the Bible, but one amazing one has to do with a woman who had been ill for twelve years. Imagine that! That might be longer than you've even been alive! When she first got sick, she went to the doctor to get medicine so she could get well. But nothing worked, so she lived—each day—with her illness. People around her were tired of hearing that she wasn't well. She was certainly tired of talking about it and tired of feeling bad. She became an outcast because of her illness; people didn't want to be around her.

But one day, she heard that Jesus the Healer was nearby, and she went out to see him. She knew other people wouldn't be glad to see her, but she trusted that Jesus could heal her and that he cared about her. She trusted that he was on her side. She thought to herself that if she could only touch his clothing as he walked by—even for half a second—she would finally be healed.

Jesus was surrounded by a big crowd, bumping and jostling against each other, when he came near to her. She reached out, maybe just barely grazing his shirt with her outstretched hand. And the moment she touched him, she was healed! She felt it immediately. But Jesus stopped in his tracks. He looked at all the people around him and asked who it was who touched his clothes. His disciples thought it was a funny question—they were in a big crowd and lots of people were knocking against Jesus. But he had felt something different when this woman reached out to him. Maybe it felt like a shock or a little jolt of energy. Jesus wanted to meet the person who had caused that!

"Who touched me?" he asked.

The woman was afraid she would be in trouble for touching Jesus. She got down on the ground and kneeled at his feet. She told him that she had been sick for a long time and how she had trusted that if she could only touch his clothes—even for a second—she would be healed.

The woman didn't need to be afraid. Jesus wasn't angry at her.

"Go in peace," he said. "Your faith has healed you."

(You can read this story in Mark 5:27–34.)

Why do you think this woman thought Jesus could heal her when none of the doctors had been able to do so?

Why do you think Jesus asked who touched him? Did he really not know?

What do you think was the first thing that woman did when she got home again?

TRY IT!

1. Close your eyes in a moment, and picture yourself in that crowd around Jesus. Think of something that troubles you, whether it's a physical problem or a friendship that's hard or a worry you have. Imagine that you gently reach out and touch Jesus's sleeve. Imagine the hurt feelings or worry or physical pain falling off you in that instant!

2. Do a "trust fall" onto your bed. You could sit up straight, with your feet dangling off the side of the bed, and let yourself flop back. Your prayer of trust could be this flopping motion.

3. Read this verse from the Bible: "I know what I am planning for you," says the LORD, "I have good plans for you, not plans to hurt you. I will give you hope and a good future" (Jeremiah 29:11, NCV).

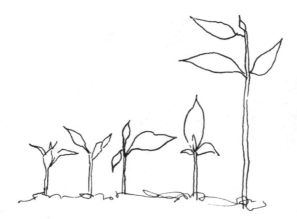

Are there any words in that verse that you like? Any that you'd like to carry along with you in your heart? Repeat them, quietly, in your mind. You might choose "hope and a future" or "I know the plans" or "not to harm you."

Gentle Jesus,
Thank you for the peace
you bring.
I trust in your love for me.
Amen.

CHAPTER 13
Breathe

Without trying or even thinking about it, we are always breathing . . . in and out, in and out. When we *inhale*, we take air into our lungs. When we *exhale*, or breathe air out of our bodies, we release a gas called carbon dioxide. Think about your respiratory system as one of your body's janitors; our lungs get rid of waste gases which would be bad for us if they were trapped inside. (As you know, bodies "take out the trash" for us in other ways too.) All day, every day, all night, every night, we take in fresh air and get rid of carbon dioxide.

gas: One of three main "states of matter": solids, liquids, and gases. Rocks, glass, and wood are solids. Water and oil are liquids, and they have no definite shape. Gases are materials that are always changing shape; helium, hydrogen, and oxygen are examples of gases.

Animals like cats and dogs have lungs and respiratory systems just like we do. You can hear a cat breathe when she purrs, and you can watch her body gently rise and fall as her lungs fill up with air and then empty again. After running around the park, a dog cools down by panting, his breathing

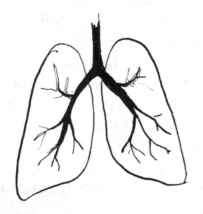

respiratory system: The web of organs and tissues in our bodies—including airways, lungs, and blood vessels—that make it possible for us to breathe.

fast, his tongue hanging out of his mouth. Animals release carbon dioxide when they exhale too.

Did you know that *all other* living things breathe too? Insects and plants—unlike people and other mammals— don't breathe in and out of their lungs. (They don't even *have* lungs!) So . . . how do they breathe?

Bugs inhale air through holes (called "spiracles") that are on the outside of their bodies. The insides of insects' bodies are kind of like sponges; when bugs breathe in through their spiracles, the inside of their bodies take the air into tiny spongelike holes. Spiracles also push out the same waste gas (carbon dioxide) that we exhale.

The way plants breathe is a little bit different. Plants breathe through tiny slits that scientists call "stomata"; their stalks, stems, and trunks are covered with them. (*Stomata* is the Greek word for "mouths.") Trees, flowers, and even blades of grass have stomata. Light causes these little slits to open, so they are usually open during the day and closed at night. But here's what's really different about the way plants breathe: while people and insects and other animals breathe carbon dioxide *out*, plants breathe it *in*, capturing it, and actually *creating* the pure air that we breathe.

Sometimes people call plants and trees "Earth's defenders" or "bio shields" because of the way they slurp up carbon dioxide and fight global warming and climate change. Too much carbon dioxide causes *global warming*, meaning that oceans and land and air heat up. This hurts life on Earth in many ways. It isn't healthy for fish to swim in a warmer ocean. When our planet gets too warm, land that used to be covered in snow and ice melts, leaving the animals and plants that need to live in cold places without a

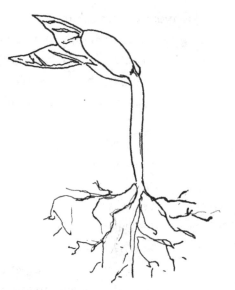

safe place to thrive. A warmer climate has natural disasters—like wildfires, droughts, and hurricanes—more often. So the fact that plants and trees capture carbon dioxide, instead of creating it, makes them heroes of the planet!

We eat the food that plants grow, like apples and carrots and even chocolate from cocoa beans. We love to look at a sunny daisy growing along the sidewalk or a willow tree sweeping the grass with its long, feathery branches. Plants give us life in other ways, too, by releasing oxygen into the air so we can breathe more freely.

Think about how all of nature breathes!

Look at a tree or at a picture of a tree. Imagine it breathing, in and out and in and out, making pure air for you to breathe.

When we feel nervous or afraid, our chests may feel tight or like something heavy is weighing down on them. At  those times, we breathe in and out very quickly, almost like a dog panting. Our hearts beat faster. We might feel unhappy or like we can't focus. But there is one simple and fast way to help us to calm down at those times. You might have guessed it . . . it's to pay attention to and control the way we are breathing.

When you want to breathe deeply, ignore what is happening around you. Try to get into a quiet place where you feel safe and cozy. Breathe in through your nose and out through your mouth. Pay attention to the way you bring air into your body and exhale it. Focus on your stomach and let the air you breathe fill up your lungs and let your belly expand or get bigger. Then, slowly, breathe out. Try to breathe out for longer than you breathed in. Maybe silently count to five as you slowly inhale and then count to seven as you exhale, letting all the air out.

In the scriptures, the Spirit of God is often described as "wind" or "breath." Spirit blows through us, fills us, and deeply calms us down. Amazingly, God's Spirit also prays for us. Romans 8: 26–27 reads, "The Spirit helps us in our weakness." It goes on to say that the Spirit feels deeply for us when we are hurting and prays for us.

What would you like God's Spirit to pray for you?

Imagine God's Spirit coming into your lungs when you inhale, filling you with pure love.

Psalm 46 tells us that God protects us (verse 1). It promises us that God will bring peace to us all (verse 9), and verse 10 is an invitation to breathe deeply.

It reads, "Be still, and know that I am God."

What might it mean to "know that God is God"?

When was a time when you felt like your breathing got too fast?

How did you slow it down?

When do you breathe most slowly and calmly?

Say the words, quietly in your mind: "Be still, and know that I am God." Let these words fill your mind with peace.

▨ ▨ ▨ ▨ ▨

TRY IT!

1. Practice "mindful breathing." This just means really paying attention to your breath, the way you draw in and release your breaths. Pay attention to the flow of air, coming into your body through your nose and then leaving your body as you breathe out of your mouth. Breathe slowly and comfortably. You may close your eyes if you like and imagine the pure air filling your lungs and traveling through your body.

2. Pray a short breath prayer. Choose two words, such as
"Be still" or "God's love" or "Peace now" and silently
repeat them, the first word on your inhale and the
second word as you breathe out. Let God's Spirit calm
you through this simple breathing prayer.

Breath of Life,
Divine Spirit,
With every breath,
please fill me up
and calm me down.
Amen.

CHAPTER 14
Cry

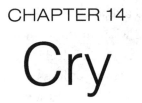

Have you ever heard someone use the phrase "a good cry" and wondered what in the world could be *good* about crying? Don't we cry when it feels like our hearts are bending and breaking from sadness or disappointment or because we are so mad we could scream? But have you ever noticed that *after* you cry, you often feel better than you did before? It's like all the stress or sadness or anger you were holding inside gets flushed out of your body through your tears.

Well, there's actually scientific proof to back that up.

Our bodies produce three different kinds of tears. The tears that keep your eyes moist and help to clear out dust are called "basal tears." "Reflex tears" are triggered when strong scents (like onions or perfume) irritate your eye. The tears that are made when you have strong feelings—whether they're happy, like when you're laughing so hard that you cry, or negative, like when you're lonely or upset—are called "emotional tears." Emotional tears have a different chemical make-up than the other kinds of tears and release chemicals that ease both physical and emotional pain. When we cry out emotional tears, our pain is numbed, our breathing becomes more regular and even, and we often feel better than we did before. Part of being a person is hurting, crying, and grieving sometimes. And our tears help us recover from these hard things.

So maybe calling it "a good cry" is not such a confusing thing to say after all.

In the book of Genesis, we learn about a woman named Hagar who, with her teenaged son, Ishmael, was experiencing homelessness. She and Ishmael were out in the desert without food, water, or shelter. When Ishmael became so weak that he could not walk, Hagar helped him lie down under a bush in the shade. Unable to move, feeling very hungry and afraid, Ishmael laid there, just crying. Hagar knew he might not survive, and she also began to weep.

But just then, an angel called to Hagar, telling her not to be afraid. (Over and over in the Bible, angels tell people not to be afraid. "Fear not" seems to be their favorite thing to say, and it's usually the first thing angels say when they appear to people!)

After telling her not to be afraid, the angel said, "Lift the boy up and take him by the hand." Hagar did that, and then she noticed a well, full of fresh water, near Ishmael. She brought him water, and he drank. The Bible doesn't say what happens next that day for Hagar and Ishmael, but we

know they both survived that terrible time. We're told, simply, that "God was with the boy as he grew up."

(You can read this story in Genesis 21:8–21.)

What do you think the angel's voice sounded like?

I wonder whether it was strong and booming, like
    thunder, or quiet, like a breeze?

*Have you ever been really thirsty and then had cool water
    to drink?*

Giving her life-saving water isn't the first time God has
noticed Hagar. Earlier in her story, when she learned that
she was pregnant with Ishmael, Hagar invented a new name
for God. She called God *El Roi*, which in the Hebrew language means, "the God Who Sees Me."

I wonder whether Hagar, alone with Ishmael, ever
    thought that El Roi no longer saw her.

*Think of a time when you wondered whether God had
    forgotten about you.*

How did that feel? How did you manage your feelings?

TRY IT!

1. Sometime, when you feel like it, come back to this page and cry a prayer to God by filling in the tear shape on this page. Write down any worries in it, or simply touch it.

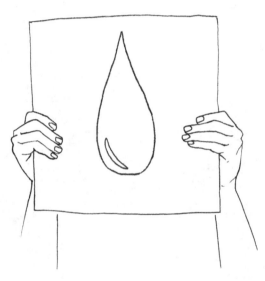

2. Write "Dear God" at the top of a piece of paper and "Amen" at the bottom of the page. Get a glass of water and sprinkle drops of water on the page; imagine the drops of water are your tears.

3. Psalm 56:8 (NLT) says, "You keep track of all my sorrows. You have collected all my tears in your bottle." The next time you cry, offer your tears as a prayer to the God who sees you. Imagine God collecting each and every one of your tears in a beautiful bottle.

God Who Sees Me,
Be with me when I cry.
Help me not to be afraid,
but to believe that you
are always with me.
Amen.

CHAPTER 15
Taste

Have you ever been to a feast? Maybe your family has big holiday dinners on Thanksgiving or Christmas or Easter Sunday. Special meals are part of many religious traditions too. Christians celebrate Holy Communion, or the Eucharist, during church services, eating bread and drinking wine or grape juice to remember Jesus and to feel close to him. Some churches offer Holy Communion every week, others less often. In early spring, Jews celebrate Passover by having a seder meal, where special foods are eaten and stories from the Bible are told.

Or maybe you've been to a wedding reception and been wowed by all the amazing food and dishes and cake. Feasts and banquets are, of course, much fancier than regular meals. The table is set more carefully. Great thought is given to decorations, to what traditions are kept, and to each guest's comfort and desires. People look forward to these special events for months in advance.

People all over the world celebrate special occasions by having feasts. There are enough holidays that are celebrated by these meals to fill this whole book. But here are a few—read on but be warned that you might get hungry!

"Fat Tuesday" is celebrated in countries like Germany and Italy, as well as in New Orleans, Louisiana, where it is called *Mardi Gras*. Fat Tuesday is always the day before Ash Wednesday when the season of Lent begins. During Lent, many Christians fast or choose to "give up" certain favorite foods so they can focus on spiritual things. But on Fat Tuesday, there are no rules. Loud music is played, people dance in the street, and folks eat as many treats as they like!

Lent: The forty-day period leading up to Easter. Some people stop eating favorite foods during that time. Others choose to focus on spiritual things by praying more often or giving money to people in need. On Easter people celebrate the resurrection of Jesus by feasting on good food, enjoying sweets, and looking for signs of new life.

Every June, in countries including Sweden, Finland, and Latvia, the brightest day of the year, or *Midsommar*, is celebrated by feasting on pickled and smoked fish, crisp bread, and berries.

The most celebrated festival in India, the Festival of Light or *Diwali*, lasts for five days. Partygoers eat stuffed pastries like samosas, fried dough, and sweets.

Nowruz, or Persian New Year, is a celebration of spring that is observed in Iran, Afghanistan, and other parts of the world. The holiday has been celebrated for more than three thousand years! The food served during Nowruz features green herbs, including basil, cilantro, parsley, and dill. Those green herbs are meant to symbolize new life and abundance. Other foods served include noodle soup, stuffed grape leaves, and many kinds of cookies.

The Korean festival *Chuseok* is a time when families gather to eat together and to thank their ancestors for a plentiful harvest. Soft rice cakes, mung bean pancakes, stir fried meat and vegetables and noodles, and fresh fruit are traditionally served.

In West Africa, particularly in the countries of Nigeria and Ghana, *Ikeji* (which means "new yam") is celebrated among the Igbo people. This is also a harvest festival where people give thanks for their farms and crops. The foods served at this feast are mostly made from—yes, you guessed it!—yams, which are like sweet potatoes.

Feasts are a way to gather together with people you love, to celebrate new beginnings, and to thank God for our blessings. When we eat together, we feel closer to each other and even closer to God. We cooperate better. We understand each other better. And, oh, it's so fun to taste so many delicious things!

■ ■ ■ ■ ■

Jesus loved telling what we call "parables" to teach people about God. A parable is a story—an everyday story about families or planting seeds or looking for lost money or other things—that has a deep spiritual meaning. He told these stories of ordinary people and events to teach us about divine truths.

Maybe Jesus told parables so that people could sit with their thoughts, listen to their hearts, and learn different things, depending on who they were. Two people hearing the same story might get two very different messages. One might learn that God forgives us, and another might realize that we need to forgive other people. Some people didn't understand Jesus's stories. Some people didn't like them. But, for those who knew and loved Jesus, these stories caught their attention, made them think, and helped them learn something about God.

One of the stories Jesus told is the "parable of the great banquet." In it, he described the kingdom of heaven as a feast. In this story, a person was hosting a fancy banquet and invited many people to come. But when it was time to sit down to dinner, no one came. Everyone who had been invited sent excuses about why they couldn't make it. The person throwing the feast then told the people who worked for him to go out into the fields and roads and invite *anyone* who'd like to come, especially people who were poor or disabled or blind! He filled all the chairs at all the tables with these new guests. People who might have gone hungry that night got to go to a fabulous party and eat that wonderful feast.

(You can read this parable in Luke 14:16–23.)

If you were the person in the parable holding the feast, what foods would you serve?

What would it feel like to invite someone over and, later, they didn't show up?

Why do you think so many people decided not to come to the feast after all?

What might this tell us about the good things God has for us?

What might this parable tell us about God's generosity?

TRY IT!

1. Plan a feast with your family and invite someone to come over and enjoy it. As you help set the table, as you help prepare the food, imagine that each action you are doing is a prayer of thanks for God's blessings. (You could use menu planning ideas from the feasts described earlier in this chapter. Is there a food you'd like to try that you've never eaten?)

2. Next time you eat, slow down and think about the miracle of that food you are tasting. If you eat a piece of fruit, slowly taste it, and imagine what had to happen to get it from being a seed to being, for example, a delicious, crunchy bite of apple in your mouth. Some-

one planted a seed, took care of a small tree, the sun
shone on it, rain watered it. As it grew, someone pruned
its branches. Then, maybe about ten years after that little
seed was planted, someone picked an apple. How did it
get from the orchard to the grocery store to your house?
Say a word of thanks for each person and each part of
the process that brought this delicious thing to you.

Thank you, Wellspring of Life,
for your generosity
and for all the good things
you give us to eat.
Bless those who are hungry,
and help me to bless them too!
Amen.

CHAPTER 16
Write

f you give a toddler a crayon, they'll probably grab it and start moving their fist around to make squiggles and loops. An older child might think for a moment and then draw something that you can tell is meant to be a face or a house or a cow. The same child, a few years later, will be writing out their ABCs and simple words, like *H-A-T* or *B-A-L-L*. When we begin to learn to read and write, we no longer need to draw a picture of something; we can say what it is we're thinking about by writing words about it.

Human beings have loved telling stories for thousands of years, with pictures and with words. Before we learned to write letters and words, early people told stories by speaking them aloud and by drawing or painting pictures. These pictures helped them to keep track of things they owned or helped them to remember what something looked or what something felt like—like after they saw a huge animal.

One underground network of caves in France, called *Grotte de Rouffignac* (sounds like *"grott duh row-fin-yak"*), has hundreds of images of woolly mammoths on its walls. Dating to the prehistoric Paleolithic period, the drawings and paintings were made tens of thousands of years ago. There

are pictures of horses, bison, rhinoceroses, as well as other designs and shapes on those walls. Early people also painted the stars they saw in the night sky. There are outlines of hands, too, at that cave in France (and in others all over the world) that seem to be like an artist's signature.

prehistoric: A time before humans wrote, and therefore for which we have no written history, such as books or letters or other documents.

Paleolithic: A time when early humans lived in caves and used very simple tools like stone axes for hunting; this period started about 2.5 million years ago and ended about 10,000 years before Jesus was born.

woolly mammoths: Extinct animals that were about the size of today's African elephants; they had very long tusks.

Like that preschooler writing their ABCs, human beings evolved and began to find better ways to record their thoughts and ideas and memories. They learned ways to make marks—lines and squiggles—on bones or on shells or in wet clay. It was the first kind of writing, and because of the invention of writing, we can learn about what happened in the past, how people lived and survived, and what it meant to be a person a long time ago. And today because we know what lines and squiggles on a page mean, we can read books, like the one you are holding right now.

The first actual writing—later than those cave pictures—was probably created because someone wanted to say something to someone who lived far away. Rather than just drawing a picture of something they wished to buy (like a sheep or a jar of olives), they began to create symbols to stand in for the sounds they used in their language when they said those things. People began to be able to write about ideas, memories, and things more complicated than buying an animal or food. People started writing about their own hardships and hopes, and they could also write about their religious beliefs.

More than two thousand years before the birth of Jesus, a poem we know as *The Epic of Gilgamesh* was written. It is one of the oldest pieces of literature, and teaches us, in a way no cave paintings could ever come close to doing, what ancient people thought about friendship, about being famous, and about death.

Imagine a world without writing.

If you had to tell someone about your life
    without using words, and only by using
    pictures, what would you draw?

Would you rather read a book that is
    told all in pictures, like a comic
    book, or a book that mostly
    uses words to tell a story?

John 1:1 reads, "In the beginning was the Word, and the Word was with God, and the Word was God." Many people who study the Bible think that when John—the person who wrote that book—used the phrase "the Word," he meant Jesus. John used that nickname for Jesus, "the Word," four times in the very first chapter of his book.

John seems to be saying that Jesus was always part of God, from the very beginning. Maybe, too, he meant that Jesus is a "Word" or is the words that tell the story of God.

In the first book of the Bible, Genesis, God *speaks* things into creation:

God said, "Let there be light!" and there was light.

God said, "Let the water under the sky be gathered to one place!" and the ocean and land were made.

God then told the land to produce plants and trees; and the earth burst into life.

And John tells us that Jesus, "the Word," was there, from the very beginning.

What is your favorite part of the creation story?

What do you think God's voice sounded like when—over and over—God said, "Let there be . . . "?

How might telling a story about something make it come to be?

What might God be calling into creation today?

In what ways might Jesus be a "word" for explaining God?

TRY IT!

1. Write a letter to God as if you are writing to a friend. You could:

- write about what happened today and how you feel about it

- talk about something you're looking forward to, like a trip or a holiday or a present

- write about your earliest memories

- make a list of ten things for which you are grateful

- write about something you'd like to understand better

- describe a goal you are working toward

- tell God all about yourself, as though God's a stranger you just met

2. Write yourself a letter from God. What might God have to say to you? What words would you like to read if you were to receive a letter from God?

3. Make and decorate a prayer box or jar, and write prayers, releasing them to the Divine when you slip your prayer in.

4. Keep a prayer journal to remember what you've asked of God or ways you've lifted your soul toward the Divine. If there are ways you feel God has responded to your prayers, write those answers down in your journal too.

Mysterious Word,
Timeless God,
speak to me,
speak through me.
Write your message of love
deep in my heart.
Amen.

CHAPTER 17
Spin

Have you ever seen a field of gigantic white turbines, spinning in the wind? Wind turbines are like huge fans, except instead of using *electricity* to create *wind*, they use *wind* to create *electricity*. Wind parks can either be built on land or in lakes and oceans. The most up-to-date turbines stand about three times as tall as the Statue of Liberty, and their blades are longer than football fields!* A single wind turbine can provide electricity for a whole town.

We refer to wind power as *solar energy*. "Solar" means related to the sun and "solar energy" means that the sun's heat and light turns into another kind of energy, the kind that can run refrigerators and air conditioners and keep the lights on in our homes.

Wind is caused when the sun heats the atmosphere and earth's surface. People have used wind energy for thousands of years. Windmills have pumped water and crushed grain. Sailors have always relied on wind to fill their sails and make their boats move. We play in the wind, blowing bubbles, flying kites, and letting breezes play songs on our porch wind chimes.

In the same way that wind makes turbines spin and boats speed and kites fly, God's Spirit—which is compared with the wind *many* times in the Bible—moves in and through us, bringing us to life. God's Spirit is as close as our breath.

---

*Tomas Kellner, "Extreme Measures: At 107 Meters, the World's Largest Wind Turbine Blade Is Longer than a Football Field. Here's What It Looks Like," GE, April 18, 2019, https://www.ge.com/news/reports/extreme-measures-107-meters-worlds-largest-wind-turbine-blade-longer-football-field-heres-looks-like.

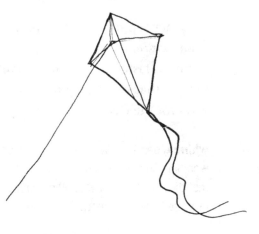

Christians believe that God chose to come to live in a *body* to express God's love for us. Jesus was a real, live, breathing person. He was a baby and then a child and then a teenager and then a grown-up. He got hungry and thirsty, just as you do. He got frustrated, just as you do. His feet hurt when he walked a long way. He danced and laughed and slept and swam. He gave his friends food to eat, healed people by touching them, and held other people close when they were sad. When he felt the Spirit moving in him, Jesus used his body to pray—just like we do.

Some people kneel when they pray; some bow their heads. Some people stretch or do yoga poses in prayer. Others dance. Others walk a labyrinth. People in many religions walk in meditation or prayer. The Buddhist teacher Thich Nhat Hanh wrote, "Walk as if you are kissing the Earth with your feet."*

** Thich Nhat Hanh, *How to Walk* (Berkeley, CA: Parallax Press, 2015), 33.*

Others spin around to pray to God. For hundreds of years, *whirling dervishes* have spun their bodies around and around, faster and faster, chanting God's name. They believe that when they pray like this, they become "doorways for the Divine."

whirling dervish: Part of the Sufi branch of Islam, a dervish—who worships God by spinning— is like a monk in the Christian religion in that they live together with other dervishes and do not marry and promise to live in poverty.

How do you move or hold your body when you pray?

In what ways is God like the sun?

In what ways is God's Spirit like the wind?

In what ways is your body like a turbine or a kite or a windmill or a boat?

When have you felt God's Spirit moving through a place, or even moving through you?

God's people have always moved their bodies in prayer. The Bible tells us that our body is a "temple of the Holy Spirit" (1 Corinthians 6:19). What might this mean? St. Paul, who wrote that verse, could have used a word like "home," saying that our bodies are the *houses* of the Holy Spirit. But he used the word "temple," showing us that our bodies are sacred; they're holy, blessed, connected to the Divine. We can use our bodies to care for others and to pray.

Psalm 149:3 says we can praise God with dancing. A prophet in the Hebrew Bible, Miriam, did just that. God had saved her people from those who were chasing after them, and Miriam "took a tambourine in her hand; and all the women went out after her with tambourines and with dancing" (Exodus 15:20). Later, King David "danced before the LORD with all his might" (2 Samuel 6:14). And when the apostle Peter, in Jesus's name, healed a disabled beggar, the newly healed man "went with them into the temple courts, walking and jumping, and praising God" (Acts 3:8 NIV).

TRY IT!

Here are a few of the ways you can move in prayer:

1. Roll down a hill or spin in a desk chair or just move around in circles in prayer. Ask God's Spirit to move in you.

2. Stand or sit up tall. Bring your hands together, as if in prayer, in front of your chest. Then sweep your arms up and above you if you are able. Imagine God's Spirit moving through you.

3. Go on a prayer walk, either outdoors or around your home. You can take a prayer walk alone or with other people. As you walk, see what grabs your attention. Could it be something that you bring to God in prayer? You could thank God for the beauty of a tree you pass or the clouds above you in the sky. You could pray for a neighbor or for a passing stranger.

Breath of the Almighty,
Spirit of Might,
Let me feel your smile
as I live and move in the body
You gave to me.
Amen.

Final Thoughts

So how does prayer work, anyway? Is it a way to be in conversation with the Divine? Is it a way to get God's attention, like throwing pebbles at someone's window because you got locked out of your house? Is it opening ourselves to God's presence? Does it change us or does it change God's mind?

I once met a woman who had been praying for something very important for many years. But, year after year, God didn't seem even to hear her prayers. She questioned God, lost her temper with God, begged God, and opened herself to the Divine presence countless times.

And she heard nothing.

"Why? Why? Why won't you do this for me?" she asked, again and again.

Finally, she heard a response that she was quite sure came from God. The words slipped into her mind, quietly and calmly. She felt immediate and deep peace.

The response was: "I'm a mystery. Can you live with that?"

"Yes," she said. And then, "I trust you."

From then on, she no longer asked for God to change the situation she'd been praying about; nothing changed, but she no longer needed things to change.

In his book on prayer, Father James Martin acknowledges that it's impossible to know how prayer works.

He writes, "I trust God hears our prayers and answers them, in some way."*

Maybe that's the best we can do, to try to trust like that, trust that your prayers are heard and answered by a mysterious God who loves you.

* * * * *

Holy Spirit,
I trust you
as I speak, sing, dance,
cry, rage, and spin
in my prayers.
Thank you for knowing my heart.
Amen.

---

* James Martin, SJ, *Learning to Pray: A Guide for Everyone* (New York: HarperOne, 2011), 111.

Acknowledgments

Thanks to my dear friend Jon Sweeney who, many years ago, wrote *Praying with Our Hands*, one of the books I've given as a gift most often in my life. It was my companion while I wrote this book. Thanks, too, to a friend I haven't yet met, Fr. James Martin, SJ, for writing *Learning to Pray*. It was another wonderful resource for me. I highly recommend both of these books on prayer.

Thank you to Wendy Claire Barrie and Milton Brasher-Cunningham for inviting me to write this book.

Thanks to Traci Smith for your friendship, prayers, and for helping me see this project over the finish line.

My thanks to Rev. Dr. Wil Gafney. Your list of names of God and titles of the Divine from *A Women's Lectionary for the Whole Church* inspired me. I used several of these names and titles in this book.

Thank you to all of my friends who pray for me: especially Dale Hanson Bourke, Susy Flory, Alethea Funck, Alison Hodgson, Keri Wyatt Kent, Mary Lewis, Andrea Nelson Le Roy, Glenys Nellist, and Caryn Rivadeneira.

Most especially, I am thankful to my mother, Dr. Myrna Grant, who has always taught me that God hears our prayers . . . and whom I found, countless times as a child, sitting on the living room sofa reading her Bible and praying when I would wake up and come downstairs for breakfast.